the
Confidence
Plan

the
Confidence
Plan

Discover
Your Confidence,
Learn to Trust Yourself Deeply,
and Step Out Boldly into a
Happier, More Fulfilled,
and Successful Life

Meridith Elliott Powell

Published and Distributed by

SOUND WISDOM
PO Box 310
Shippensburg, PA 17257-0310
717-530-2122

info@soundwisdom.com
www.soundwisdom.com

ISBN 13: 978-1-64095-431-1
ISBN 13 eBook: 978-1-64095-432-8

For Worldwide Distribution, Printed in the U.S.A.
1 2 3 4 5 6 / 26 25 24 23 22

Contents

Confidence: What Is It, and Why Does It Matter?

The modern world moves quickly. Faster than ever, new technologies are emerging, the economy is shifting, and the pace of life is increasing.

Sometimes it can feel like a never-ending storm of playing catch-up. There are some who might feel overwhelmed by the perceived pressure to keep up or be afraid of taking risks that might set them back further. And yet, there are others who have a deep inner knowing that despite the storm they are in, they can navigate themselves back to safety and blue skies.

That inner knowing is *confidence*. When we have confidence in ourselves and our abilities, we can weather any storm in our professional and personal lives and know that we'll come through better and stronger on the other side.

WHAT IS CONFIDENCE?

Confidence is the steadfast trust and belief that you can rely on something. When we apply that to the kind of confidence you'll be learning in this book, confidence is about *trusting and believing in yourself.*

When you are confident, you believe in your own skills and abilities—even when things don't work on the first try. Your confidence gives you the strength to persevere and keep trying until you succeed. It's the calm response of "I can do this" any time your fear or anxiety raises doubt in your mind.

Confidence gives you the voice to speak up for the things you believe in, to accept and appreciate your failures, and to follow the clear vision you have for yourself—even if it means going against the current.

The best thing about confidence is that every aspect is a teachable skill that you can learn, grow, and develop.

WHY DOES IT MATTER?

To put it simply, confident people are more successful and more resilient.

Whether your goals are to sell more, to be promoted, to switch careers, or simply to be more fulfilled in your life, confidence plays an important role in each of these. People want to hire confident employees, buy from confident salespersons, and follow confident leaders. It's a quality that we as humans are naturally drawn to and a trait that most successful people have.

When you trust your skills and abilities, you move *toward* opportunities rather than hesitating or waiting for everything to align perfectly. Because of this, confident people end up taking more risks, which improves their success rate. The confident mindset understands that mistakes are an inevitable part of learning and that they provide valuable knowledge for the future. So when they make mistakes, people with confidence learn from them and keep trying until they succeed.

With this resilience, you don't become a victim in the narrative of your life but instead remain the hero regardless of the outcome of a situation. Because of your deep understanding and trust in yourself, you recognize that failures are situational and temporary: your skills and abilities will eventually bring you success.

HOW DO YOU LEARN TO BE CONFIDENT?

As with most things, you'll need a plan and lots of practice.

This book is designed to be your guide on the path of finding your own confidence to lead you to a happier, more fulfilled, and successful life.

So let's get to work!

CHAPTER EXERCISE: WHAT DOES CONFIDENCE MEAN TO YOU?

Now that we've covered everything that confidence enables you to do and the different presentations of confidence, write down in a few sentences what confidence means to you.

_____

_____

_____

_____

_____

_____

_____

_____

_____

_____

_____

_____

_____

_____

_____

_____

_____

_____

_____

_____

_____

Chapter

2

Creating the Foundation and Committing to Becoming More Confident

All great things are built with solid foundations. Confidence is no different.

Without a firm foundation in the fundamentals of confidence, you might outwardly appear to be confident and possess the skills that come with it, but you're vulnerable to toppling over when adversity strikes.

Take your time developing these foundational skills of confidence. These are the roots that will keep you grounded and focused along your journey.

THE FOUNDATIONS OF CONFIDENCE

The confident mindset is built upon three essential building blocks. In this book, you'll learn additional skills and techniques to build your confidence further, but they all rely on these foundational components.

1. Believe that confidence can be learned.

Your life experiences up to this point have contributed to how much confidence you currently have, but that does not mean you're limited to that amount. Confidence is a skill that you can learn at any time, any age, and anywhere.

To gain or grow it requires you to believe that it is a *skill*, and all skills can be learned. This fundamental belief will help you persevere through any challenges that arise in building your confidence skills.

2. Have a growth mindset.

A growth mindset is the belief that your skills and abilities can grow and develop through learning and practice. Once you believe that confidence can be learned, you are already exercising your growth mindset!

The opposite of this is a fixed mindset, which is believing that your abilities are predetermined so no matter how hard you try, you can't learn new skills or improve your current ones. A fixed mindset leads to self-victimization and believing that things happen *to* you, rather than knowing you can make things happen *for* you.

With a growth mindset, you can reclaim your power and learn any skill—just like you're doing now by reading this book.

3. *Know your path.*

A clear vision and purpose will keep you focused when you don't know which direction to go or when it feels like you aren't going anywhere.

This book will teach you the essential skills in building your confidence arsenal, but it's up to you to decide how they will best be used in the vision you hold for yourself and your future. Take the time to explore where you would be and what you would be able to do if you were more confident. That vision will be your fuel when the path seems unclear.

COMMITTING TO BECOMING MORE CONFIDENT

Now that you have the foundations to begin your confidence journey and a handbook to guide you there, are you ready to commit to the process?

You might be asking, *What am I committing to?* As we learned in chapter 1, confidence is a steadfast trust in *yourself*, so by committing to becoming more confident, you are making a commitment to yourself to be your own advocate, to create opportunities for yourself, and to persevere when the process gets difficult.

This commitment will be an affirmation of your resilience—a celebratory piece of evidence that you can overcome any hardship and achieve your goals.

CHAPTER EXERCISE:
DEFINE YOUR VISION

If you want to feel confident in your vision, purpose, and values, then you need to be able to clearly define what these are. This vision will keep you focused during difficult times and help guide you in your decisions.

In the space below, answer the following questions: What does a fulfilled version of your life look like, and what keeps you motivated to achieve it?

_____

_____

_____

_____

_____

_____

_____

_____

_____

_____

_____

_____

_____

_____

_____

_____

_____

_____

_____

_____

_____

Chapter

3

Embracing Fear and Failure

What keeps you from pursuing the things you want? What stops you from jumping into new experiences? Fear is an emotion designed to keep us safe, but it can be debilitating when we let it control us. Each time we avoid taking action out of fear, we give it a little more power over us and limit our potential for success.

Instead, learning how to embrace your fear and use it as a tool can build your confidence and create a more fulfilling and successful life.

WHERE DO OUR FEARS COME FROM?

Fear is triggered by any threat of physical, emotional, or psychological harm, whether it's real or imagined. Fear is also learned—and we can learn to be afraid of anything.

A lot of our fears are from learned experiences. When we've been hurt physically, emotionally, or psychologically, our mind remembers the pain and tries to warn us of things that look similar. The problem is that our mind is so proactive about protecting us that it often points out threats that aren't very likely or aren't dangerous at all. Over time, letting our fear have control creates a very limited existence.

Fortunately, you can teach yourself how to embrace your fear and quiet the imagined fears and anxieties that keep you from moving forward. When you have control over your fear, you can take action and achieve the things you want.

EMBRACING FEAR

The first step in embracing your fear is to understand that fear is a positive, helpful tool. Sometimes we think that ignoring our fear will help us power through and move forward, but things that are ignored have a tendency of only getting louder until they are heard.

Instead of ignoring your fear, *embrace it.* Learn to listen to your fear and acknowledge it, then decide how *you* want to act. It's okay to listen to your fear. Think of fear as a tool that informs you of possible threats so you can devise a plan, mitigate risk, and increase your chance of success.

The difference between embracing your fear and being ruled by it is which entity has the power to take action. When fear is in power, it tends to prevent action. When you choose to embrace your fear and be informed by it, *you* are in control and *you* have the power to take action.

A NUMBERS GAME

The people who embrace their fears and failures tend to be the most successful. Why is that? Well, it's a numbers game.

We tend to view failure as a finality, so we try to avoid it. In doing so, we end up avoiding opportunities while we wait for things to align, for us to be more prepared, or for another opportunity with less risk. This limits the chance of failure, but it also limits our chance of success.

Failure is just a lesson on your way to success. When you learn to embrace it, you pursue more opportunities and inevitably have more success.

CHAPTER EXERCISE: PUSHING PAST YOUR FEAR

Write down ten things you avoid doing out of fear. Starting small, choose one item to push through and conquer.

Each time you succeed and conquer another anxiety, celebrate! Give yourself a reward for pushing past your fear. The more you practice embracing your fear and getting out of your comfort zone, the easier it will get. It starts with the first step.

_____

_____

_____

_____

_____

_____

_____

_____

_____

_____

_____

_____

_____

_____

_____

_____

_____

_____

_____

Chapter

Understanding Yourself

Confidence comes from knowing who you are and trusting that person completely. This trust can't exist without a deep understanding of yourself. Why do you react the way you do in certain situations? What inspires and motivates you? What fuels your anxieties?

Knowing the answers to these questions helps us understand ourselves, how we fit into the world around us, and how to use that knowledge to be more confident.

TUNING IN TO SELF-AWARENESS

Self-awareness is about seeing yourself clearly—understanding your strengths, weaknesses, motivations, anxieties, and reactions. It's about understanding all the things that make you a unique individual and knowing where these traits come from. With self-awareness, we're more confident and creative.

Here are some ways to cultivate and tune in to your own self-awareness:

1. *Take time for self-reflection.*

Set aside time to get in touch with your emotions and understand them. The better you understand your emotions, the better you will be at controlling them and understanding the emotions of others.

2. *Analyze your reactions.*

Sometimes we react in ways that are surprising—even to us. These moments are opportunities to gain a deeper understanding of ourselves and to become more aware of the origins of our emotions.

When you find yourself reacting emotionally or in a way that surprises you, take time to analyze the situation by asking yourself a series of "why" questions. *Why did I raise my voice like that? Why was I frustrated? Why does it matter so much to me?* At the end of your questions, you're likely to find insight that can give you a deeper understanding of yourself and help you avoid losing control in the future.

3. *Get trusted opinions.*

There are some things that we can't objectively measure in ourselves, like our communication style and body language. Getting the trusted opinion of people who have your best interests in mind can help you gain insight into how others perceive you. You might be made aware of something you didn't know about yourself, or you might not. But an objective point of view builds your self-awareness so you can learn how others' perceptions align with or differ from your own view of self.

EMBRACE YOUR PERSONALITY AND YOUR PAST

Being completely confident and understanding yourself means addressing and embracing the things that make us who we are, including those things that are not in our control.

Rather than trying to manipulate your personality, understand your tendencies and use that knowledge as empowerment. Rather than hiding from your past or ignoring it, take time to understand the events that made you *you* and apply that insight in your pursuit of success.

Understanding yourself means having a complete and full vision of all the things that make you who you are—imperfections and all. This understanding is powerful: it lets you walk into any room, any situation, or any conversation with complete confidence. There is no reason to fear any shadows or parts of yourself that you can't control. There's no power that anyone else can have over you because you have a deep inner knowing that you are constant and cannot be changed. *That* is empowering.

CHAPTER EXERCISE: TAKE FIVE

Take five minutes to "interview" yourself: What made you happy this week? What are you most proud of? Was there a moment you wished you acted differently? Let your mind naturally choose follow-up questions and "why" questions to know and understand yourself better.

Set a time to check in with yourself once a week and gain a deeper understanding of your motivations, your reactions, and where you spend your time.

Chapter

5

Knowing and Embracing Your Strengths and Weaknesses

Having a full understanding of your strengths and weaknesses helps you focus your energy on creating opportunities from either of these. With your strengths, you can find greater success pursuing projects that play to your natural talents and abilities. And having a clear view of your weaknesses can help you determine which skills to grow and develop next.

IDENTIFY YOUR STRENGTHS AND WEAKNESSES

First, identify what your strengths and weaknesses are. To do this, you must be completely honest about what you do well...and what you do not do so well. Be as objective as possible and understand that everything is a skill that can be learned, developed, and improved.

Remember, many of your current strengths probably started out as weaknesses. So too can your current weaknesses develop into strengths.

To help you identify your strengths and weaknesses, it might be useful to ask a trusted mentor, colleague, or friend what they think. This will often provide additional insight and objectivity that can be used to inform your plan of action.

PLAY TO YOUR STRENGTHS

Analyze the areas in which you are strong, and find opportunities to let these strengths shine. This might mean taking on projects where your expertise is highly valued and appreciated or finding opportunities to share your strength in mentoring or teaching others. Not only is it more efficient to do work that plays to your natural abilities, but it also tends to be more enjoyable and rewarding.

TACKLE YOUR WEAKNESSES

Rather than being afraid of or insecure about the weaknesses you've identified, take pride in the process of learning and growing. This knowledge allows you to choose which skills you want to grow and pursue. Focus on any skills that can be applied to your key objectives, and make a plan to improve them through reading books, taking a course, hiring a coach, or practicing in situations outside your comfort zone.

The more you push past your perceived limitations and tackle your weaknesses head-on, the faster you can expand your skills and grow your list of strengths.

SEPARATING SKILL FROM SELF-WORTH

A confident person knows that their self-worth comes from more than what they do and what they are good at. Once you can see everything as a skill that can be learned, then you can detach it from your own self-worth.

This allows you to have a full understanding of your strengths and weaknesses and view feedback and criticism as helpful tools to aid in the goal of understanding yourself so that you can grow your skill set even more.

CHAPTER EXERCISE: STRENGTHS AND WEAKNESSES IN ACTION

Make a list of five things you're great at (strengths) and five things you wish you could improve (weaknesses).

Using the ideas in this chapter, brainstorm a way you can utilize each strength in an upcoming project and a way to grow and expand your skills for each weakness.

Pick one of each and make a schedule to pursue them.

_____

_____

_____

_____

_____

_____

_____

_____

_____

_____

_____

_____

_____

_____

_____

_____

_____

_____

Chapter

Quitting the Comparison Game

Confidence is being rooted in who you really are. Once you start spending energy comparing yourself to others, your competition, or even to your own expectation of who you think you should be, you lose sight of your own unique journey. Instead, keep your focus on your path and the continuous progress you're making.

EVERYONE'S CONFIDENCE LOOKS DIFFERENT

It's not about being the loudest in the room, dominating the panel, or introducing yourself to everyone at the party. As a society, we tend to confuse extroversion with confidence. The truth is, the most extroverted person can still lack self-confidence.

Just as you're unique and distinct as an individual, your confidence is too. Learn to embrace your uniqueness and exhibit your own style of confidence. When you're connected to the core of who you are, you can let your true self shine.

PRACTICE SELF-COMPASSION

Don't let your inner critic tear you down. Comparing ourselves to others or to the unattainable perfectionist ideals we might hold for ourselves is limiting. More often than not, we end up doing less and being less successful because we're waiting for everything (including ourselves) to be perfect.

Confidence is not about being perfect, or even about always *feeling* confident. It's about knowing who you are and accepting that person completely. This can be achieved only when you practice self-compassion.

Be your own champion, celebrate your successes, accept your mistakes, and speak to yourself with the kind of care and compassion you would give a loved one.

BLOCK OUT HARMFUL MESSAGES

In addition to idealized images in media and advertising, we exist in the age of social media, where we can find curated versions of the lives of celebrities, influencers, and our peers. It's easy to think that these individuals have their lives more put together than we do, but don't forget that everyone experiences bad days, self-doubt, and the voice of their own inner critic.

Block out any harmful or distracting messages. This might mean gentle reminders of self-compassion when you start unfairly comparing yourself to an image in the media, or it might mean avoiding a media channel altogether. Whatever keeps you focused on your confident path forward and away from the snares of comparison is worth it.

TURN COMPETITION INTO COLLABORATION

Once you separate your self-worth and stop comparing your success to others', you can admire your competition and be more open to collaborating. You might find that the people you admire most have a mutual admiration for your unique skills. It first takes the confidence to view competitors positively and open the door to collaboration.

CELEBRATE *YOU*

Comparing yourself to others and letting your inner critic rule your monologue and perspective takes away from *celebrating you.* Your unique version of confidence cannot exist anywhere except through you. That's something worth celebrating! Stop the comparison game and allow the rest of the world to see the unique experience that only you can bring.

CHAPTER EXERCISE: CREATE AN AFFIRMATION

Confidence is a journey that goes sideways from time to time. It's important to have a plan when your inner critic tries to tell you that you aren't good enough. To prevent your inner critic from taking control, create a positive affirmation to respond immediately.

It might sound like "Everyone has their own journey, and this is part of mine." Or, "It doesn't matter what other people are doing; I'm on my own unique path."

Find a positive affirmation for yourself and use it to respond whenever you start to hear your inner critic.

Chapter

Creating a Vision
for Your Life

If you don't know where you want to go, it's impossible to create a path to get there.

Once you have a clear vision for your life, you can start to fill in the details of what you need to know or learn to get there. While these questions might seem generic or frivolous, don't skip this step! Often we get so caught up in the momentary successes or everyday tasks that we lose sight of the direction we want to go, and when we finally look up, we wonder how we got where we are. Creating a vision for your life keeps you focused and moving forward toward your larger goals.

WHAT DO YOU WANT?

It's a simple question, but it can be hard to pinpoint our desires when we take the time to think about it. This is different from the things we think we *should* do and separate from any outside opinion. What are the things that give you joy and a sense of fulfillment in your personal and professional life?

WHERE DO YOU SEE YOURSELF?

When answering this, be sure to create a vision that really speaks to the desires you've identified for yourself rather than short-lived accomplishments or temporary pleasures. The closer you can get to your core desires in your vision for your life, the more fulfilled you'll be when you get there.

For example, years ago I worked my way up the corporate ladder to attain the job I had dreamed of. I was offered an executive title, a corner office, membership to a country club, and a six-figure salary with bonuses. It was everything I thought I wanted…until I got it.

When I learned that I had been selected for the position, I felt a rush of excitement, then immediate dread. I realized that now that I had the role, I didn't want it. The responsibility of relocating, spending my life in meetings, and giving up aspects of my personal life to put in the long hours and weekends the position required would not fulfill me.

Because I didn't set out with a clear vision for my life, I had moved up the corporate ladder and ended up in a position that didn't leave me fulfilled. It required a reevaluation of my life and my desires, leaving the company, and starting all over again to build the vision I had for my life.

MAP OUT YOUR VISION AND PURPOSE

To avoid finding yourself in a position like I did, take the time now to map out a clear vision and purpose for both your professional and personal ambitions—with notable landmark objectives along the way. Put yourself in charge of the direction of your life so you can move forward with intent and confidence as you navigate your life.

CHAPTER EXERCISE: CREATE VISION AND PURPOSE STATEMENTS

Create a Vision Statement

Describe what you want your life to look like in five years. What role will you hold professionally? Who will be in your personal life? What does your financial, social, and physical world look like?

Reflect on these questions and craft a 2–3 sentence vision statement that will help guide you in times of decision or doubt.

_____

_____

_____

_____

_____

_____

_____

_____

_____

_____

_____

_____

_____

_____

_____

_____

_____

Create a Purpose Statement

Your purpose statement acts as a personal mission statement. Think of the vision you've created for your life and the core desire that fuels and motivates you to accomplish it. Why are you pursuing this vision? Consolidate your answer into one concise mission; this is your purpose statement.

_____

_____

_____

_____

_____

_____

_____

_____

_____

_____

_____

_____

_____

_____

_____

_____

_____

_____

_____

_____

_____

_____

_____

_____

Chapter

8

Getting Real with Every Area of Your Life

Having a full grasp on your reality is crucial to navigating the world with complete confidence. When confidence isn't grounded in reality, it can bring serious consequences.

To avoid this, you must continue to practice and maintain your skills instead of "winging it," set realistic goals for yourself, be selective in saying "yes," and face your problems head-on rather than avoiding them.

DON'T "WING IT"

Overconfidence is not confidence. When you trust your skills beyond their capacity, you can set yourself up for devastating failure that is completely preventable.

Don't rely on "winging it" once you are confident in your skill set. Take the time to prepare, maintain, and refine your skills to continue on a path of success.

CREATE REALISTIC GOALS

There will be many milestones and landmarks along the path to accomplishing your vision for your life. Sometimes when we set these goals too far apart from each other, they can seem harder to reach, take more time, and make us feel discouraged. That's not to say that these goals are unattainable, but it's important to create milestones along the way.

Break up your objectives into smaller, more realistic goals that you can achieve in a manageable amount of time. This will help keep you motivated, prevent feelings of discouragement, and fuel you with the momentum of consistent accomplishment.

DON'T BE AFRAID TO SAY "NO"

Another trap we set for ourselves sometimes is saying "yes" to too many commitments. This can leave us drained and unfocused as we allocate precious time and energy to projects that don't help us actualize our vision for our life.

Be selective in saying "yes" to things, and don't be afraid to say "no." Choose to spend your energy and time on things that are fulfilling, manageable, and relevant to your larger goals.

FACE YOUR PROBLEMS

By now you've probably realized that the things we generally see as negatives—like fear, failure, or weakness—are best dealt with by embracing them and tackling them head-on.

This philosophy also applies to our problems. When we avoid our problems, it's the same as letting them have control—and the consequences can be more severe the longer we put them off.

Face your problems and take control. Focus on making small steps forward to work your way toward victory. Your problems will not go away on their own, but you can either let them haunt you or choose to conquer them and move forward confidently.

THE MAGIC OF GETTING REAL

When you choose to get real with every aspect of your life, there's nothing lurking in the shadows to haunt you and there's no lingering sense of dread or anxiety. Confidence is the freedom from these feelings—a freedom that can be accomplished only by inspecting your life in every nook and cranny and solving each messy detail one step at a time.

CHAPTER EXERCISE: A PERSONAL INSPECTION

Take time to inspect every area of your life and identify any problems you've been avoiding. Are there any skills that need to be refined or maintained? Are there problems you've been putting off or projects you've said "yes" to that you wish you hadn't?

Make a list of all these items, and create a plan to address each one. Set small, measurable, and realistic goals to conquer each item one at a time. Once you have a plan of action, you have won control over any problems and can move forward with a confidence grounded in reality.

_____

_____

_____

_____

_____

_____

_____

_____

_____

_____

_____

_____

_____

_____

_____

_____

The Confidence Plan

_____

_____

_____

_____

_____

_____

_____

_____

_____

_____

_____

_____

_____

_____

_____

_____

_____

_____

_____

_____

_____

_____

_____

_____

Chapter

Focusing on Progress
Rather Than the End Goal

What we choose to focus on will influence the ultimate direction of our journey. When we choose to focus only on our end goal, we lose sight of the process and the progress in between. With this frame of mind, the only way to satisfy ourselves is to always be chasing a new peak with the goal of feeling accomplished and fulfilled when we reach the summit.

Since most of our time is spent along the journey of achieving our goals, this approach isolates our sense of accomplishment and achievement to very brief moments of time. However, when we train ourselves to focus on the progress rather than the goal, we develop a greater sense of fulfillment and overall accomplishment in our lives.

CELEBRATE SHOWING UP

Anyone who has tried a new diet, quit smoking, or learned a new language knows that good habits can be achieved only by showing up every day. In fact, that's usually the hardest part.

Take time to notice and appreciate your willpower to push through the little things that move you toward accomplishing your goals—things like waking up early to get to the gym or taking an online course on your lunch break to learn a new skill.

These moments in between make up the majority of our time. Spend these moments wisely and take time to celebrate the accomplishment of showing up each day.

APPRECIATE THE JOURNEY

A win is a win, no matter how big or small.

It's easy to look back at the milestones of our lives and notice the big accomplishments, but it's important to acknowledge the journey and the little successes we've had along the way. Take time to reflect on your own journey, and be proud of the things you've accomplished. Look at the new skills you've developed and the new habits you've incorporated into your life. Look at the hobbies and things you do that give you joy and inspiration. These are things to be excited about—things that make the journey worthwhile.

THINK OUTSIDE THE GOAL

Setting goals isn't everything. The most important aspect of achieving your life's vision is the process.

Most of our time is spent on our way to achieving our goals. If we focus our attention solely on the peak we want to conquer, we'll miss out on the stunning views along the way. Enjoy the process and the path on the way to your goals and you'll find a deeper and richer sense of fulfillment.

CHAPTER EXERCISE: VIEW FROM THE TOP

Look back on your journey to one year ago. How far have you progressed toward your goals? What new skills or knowledge have you gained along the way? What personal accomplishments have you achieved?

Make a list of these accomplishments and take time to reward yourself for them.

Then, schedule a time each year, quarter, or month to take inventory and look back on your journey. Celebrate the gradual and consistent progress you're making each and every day.

_____

_____

_____

_____

_____

_____

_____

_____

_____

_____

_____

_____

_____

_____

_____

_____

Chapter

Condition Yourself for Change

It's not a matter of *if* change will happen but *when* change will happen—and the most confident people are prepared and ready to act when it does.

If you're constantly reacting to the world, its changes, and its uncertainties, it's impossible to move through your life confidently. Without being centered in yourself and your purpose, the winds of change can sweep you up, wear you down, and drop you off in a desert void of connections, resources, or lifelines.

To avoid that state of chaos and navigate the world and its uncertainties with confidence, we condition ourselves to be ready for change.

CHANGE = OPPORTUNITY

So often we link change with uncertainty. But when we reframe our perspective to see change as an *opportunity,* the uncertainty of not knowing what comes next can be the key to disruption. Disruption can't take place in the mundane: it *thrives* on change. And oftentimes, disruption is the key ingredient to taking you and your career to the next level.

Condition your mindset to welcome change as the opportunity you've been waiting for, and learn to leverage it as the disruption you need.

ANTICIPATE CHANGE; DON'T REACT

If you know anything about surfing (or if you've seen *Point Break*), you know that you can't catch a wave once it's already arrived. You sit and wait, watching the waves form on the horizon, letting the small waves break, and anticipating the big wave to come. When you see it coming, you start your momentum early before it reaches you. And once it breaks, you're in the perfect position to stand up and ride it all the way to shore.

If you're reacting to change, you're already behind. Even if your reaction is perfectly executed, you're too late. The winds of change are fast and fierce, and if you're not on the first gust, there's someone else who's already taken your place.

Anticipate change and make it a point to be aware of the trends in your marketplace, industry, and organization. Proactively look for change and be ready to spot it on the horizon so you can see it coming.

CHANGE IS A MUSCLE

The more you think about, talk about, and anticipate change, the more conditioned for it you'll be when it arrives. Like all muscles, change needs to be conditioned and exercised to serve a variety of purposes:

- **Flexibility:** Be adaptable, nimble, and ready to use your skills in creative ways.
- **Strength:** Have the strength to push through obstacles.
- **Endurance:** Possess the stamina to stay in the game once you're in. Keep your resources, energy, and schedule balanced so you can last to the finish line.

Even in moments and seasons of consistency, you want to keep these muscles toned and conditioned so they're ready to use.

CHAPTER EXERCISE: S.C.E.P.T.I.C. ANALYSIS

To condition and prepare yourself for the changes ahead, take 30 minutes each quarter to note the current state and trends in each of these areas:

- Society
- Competition
- Economics
- Politics
- Technology
- Industry
- Customers

Take notes on your observations in one place so you can spot any upcoming trends or changes ahead. This will give you the opportunity to disrupt the system, rather than being disrupted in the process.

_____

_____

_____

_____

_____

_____

_____

_____

_____

_____

_____

The Confidence Plan

_____

_____

_____

_____

_____

_____

_____

_____

_____

_____

_____

_____

_____

_____

_____

_____

_____

_____

_____

_____

_____

_____

_____

_____

_____

_____

_____

_____

_____

_____

_____

_____

Chapter

Know and Use
Your Core Values

The difference between being a confident decision-maker and an indecisive follower lies in staying true to your core values. Your core values are the fundamental beliefs that determine your behavior and dictate your course of action. These are the tenets that keep you grounded and focused in your daily decision-making *and* in the greatest moments of adversity.

WHAT DO YOU STAND FOR?

To find the core values that define your life's passion and direction, it takes a deep investigation into who you are and what drives you. What are your values? What do you believe in? What are your non-negotiable, "do not cross" lines?

The answers to these questions will help you narrow down the scope of your core values, but these ideas will need to be further distilled to become the actionable core values you will fight for no matter what.

Once you take the time to identify your core values, you are well on your way to walking with complete confidence in the world, unshakeable and centered in your purpose.

DECIDE WITH INTENTION

When you're rooted in your core values, decisions are simple. Instead of questioning possibilities, weighing outcomes, or flipping a coin, everything is simply a question of what aligns with your core values. You're empowered by your own inner knowing to make the best decision for you and your journey.

INTEGRITY: ALIGN YOUR ACTIONS WITH YOUR WORDS

Confidence and integrity are intertwined, and their deepest point of connection is in your core values. Integrity is staying true to your values, even when you're facing great influence, power, or temptation. These values are the definition of who you are.

When your actions are aligned with your core values, it doesn't matter who's watching or who knows about what you're doing. You do not need credit or recognition because you're doing the right thing for yourself.

Align your actions with your words, and be consistent with your follow-through. People remember when you do something you say you'll do…and they also remember when you don't. Follow through with your actions and promises, and hold true to your core values.

BE EMPOWERED BY YOUR CORE VALUES

Having a deep understanding of who you are and what you stand for allows you to exude confidence and navigate your life with integrity. You're free from needing to please anyone; instead, you're empowered by an unshakeable foundation to guide you along your path of confidence.

CHAPTER EXERCISE: DEFINE YOUR CORE VALUES

Make a list of the qualities you value most in life. Think about the traits you admire in yourself and the qualities you possessed in your proudest moments. Think about your vision and purpose and the reasons why you do what you do. Think freely and write any words that come to mind.

1. Circle any items that are non-negotiable— qualities that you absolutely believe in and cannot accept a life without. Of those items circled, choose the strongest three that resonate with who you are as a person.

2. Now, attach a verb to each of these three qualities to make it *actionable*. (For example, "Honesty" could be "Living in Honesty," or "Peace" could be "Promoting Peace.")

Once you have three actionable core values, write them down and put them in a place where you will see them every day. Keep these values in mind in your daily decisions to live a full life that reflects your core values.

Chapter

Build Your Network

Building a network can change your life, and it's much easier than you might think. When you have a solid network, you feel empowered—even in the areas outside your expertise because you have external support, a web of people who can be a resource or help you find a resource when you're in need.

Having the confidence to network can help you build, grow, and develop authentic relationships. *You don't have to do it all by yourself.*

HOW TO BUILD YOUR NETWORK

Whether you're shy and introverted or known as the "life of the party," it's important to apply some helpful tips to make the most of your networking strategy. Remember, being your authentic self will allow you to connect with people in a genuine way. If you try to be someone you're not, people will be able to sense it and won't be inclined to help you. Be confident in who you are. *That* is your most captivating quality.

MAKE A DEPOSIT
BEFORE YOU WITHDRAW

No one enjoys feeling like they're being used for their position, connections, or resources. When growing your network, invest into it long before you need it. Make yourself available and useful, offer your skills and services, and connect others within your network. Just as your bank account can be overdrawn if you withdraw more than you deposit, so can the people in your network if you take more than you contribute.

ASK FOR HELP

Don't be too proud or afraid to ask for help. Being confident means that you know you're not the best at everything and that's completely okay. Be open and honest with others about the skills you're looking to develop, the resources you need, and the kinds of companies you're looking to work with.

People are usually happy to connect two people in their own network, and an introduction can save the time of doing the research yourself or waiting for the right person to come along.

ONE CONVERSATION AWAY

Pushing yourself out of your comfort zone to build a strategic network can be hard at first, but remember: each person, each conversation, and each connection can be the one opportunity to open the door that solves your biggest challenge.

Building your network can bring unbelievable results, and one simple conversation can change your life.

CHAPTER EXERCISE: BUILDING YOUR NETWORKS

Your Internal Network (Part I): Think of the people you work with on a daily basis. How well do you know them? Do you talk to them only when you need something? Invest in your immediate network and get to know your colleagues better to foster a mutually beneficial relationship. You might discover hidden talents or valuable skills that can be helpful in collaboration.

1. **Your Internal Network (Part II):** Think of the people in your organization or company who can help you grow your career, do your job more effectively, or support your department's efforts. Make a goal to connect with someone new outside of your department each month.

2. **Your Resource Network:** Think of the skills you'd like to develop, your areas of weakness, or complementary skills to yours that can help propel you forward. Do you know anyone who might be a good resource for these? Has anyone offered to introduce you to someone who can assist? Look for opportunities to connect with people who can help you fill in the gaps.

_____

_____

_____

_____

_____

_____
_____
_____
_____
_____
_____
_____
_____
_____
_____
_____
_____
_____
_____
_____
_____
_____
_____
_____
_____
_____
_____
_____
_____
_____
_____
_____
_____
_____
_____

Chapter

Reward Action

It's hard to stay motivated when you don't enjoy the work. When we find our work exciting and challenging and feel recognized for the work we're doing, we usually end up being more successful too. The key to staying motivated toward your goals is to *reward action.*

ACTION > ACCOMPLISHMENT

The road to success doesn't have a 100 percent win rate. In fact, there are usually *a lot* of learning experiences along the way that would not be classified as "wins." That's why valuing our actions over our accomplishments gives us the stamina that long-term success requires and rewards the behavior that will actually get us there.

When we reward accomplishments or withhold rewards until we cross the finish line, we often experience a brief surge in motivation that fades before we reach our goal. Not only can this make the last leg of the journey quite grueling, but it also trains our minds to immediately find a new objective to give us that rush of motivation again. In this fluctuating dynamic, we miss out on the joy of the journey and the sustained motivation that comes from rewarding action.

WHICH ACTIONS TO REWARD

The goal of rewarding action is to celebrate the practice and process of developing the good habits that you can keep for life. The certificate of achievement at the end of a course will not bring you success, but the practice you developed of finishing assignments after work, studying on your lunch break, or organizing weekend study groups to complete the course contribute to intangible skills like drive and resilience that can help you succeed in any field.

If you want to grow your network, reward yourself each time you step out of your comfort zone and strike up a conversation with someone new. If you want to write a novel, reward yourself for showing up and writing each day—even if you write only one good sentence. These are actions. These are practices. And these are the skills that will contribute to your success in whatever you set your eyes on.

DON'T RELY ON OTHERS TO REWARD YOU

It's easy to fall into the trap of thinking, *If I work hard enough, someone will notice and reward me.* I know I have. Years ago, I thought that my passion and commitment would speak for themselves and my hard work would automatically be rewarded with opportunities and promotions. But the truth is, those opportunities came only when I created them for myself.

Having confidence releases you from the pressure of needing to perform for anyone else in order to be rewarded. It also guards you from potential feelings of bitterness or resentment. It's a great quality to take pride in your work, but do it for *you*.

Only you know your path. Reward yourself for each step forward you take.

CHAPTER EXERCISE: REWARDING ACTION

What's a big goal you're currently working toward? Make a list of the actions you need to take to achieve that goal. Break down your action steps into smaller actions you can accomplish a few times a week or daily.

Choose a couple to reward regularly through a compliment, small treat, reward of time (ten-minute walk, extra time to sleep in), or a monetary reward like a fund that is added up at the end of the week or month for a bigger reward.

Find ways to reward your actions regularly and give yourself the recognition and validation you deserve. You've earned it!

_____

_____

_____

_____

_____

_____

_____

_____

_____

_____

_____

_____

_____

_____

Chapter

Focus Outward

Focusing outward is a conscious choice to see beyond ourselves. Sometimes, whether through self-consciousness, self-centeredness, or just anxiety about our own lives, we lose sight of the outside world and get caught up inside our minds.

If you're someone who experiences social anxiety or is nervous being in front of people, this tendency might express itself as worrying too much about what other people think of you. If you're nervous or anxious in social situations, your inner distractions might present themselves as interrupting conversations or talking at length. Whatever inward focus you might momentarily have takes energy away from being confident in yourself and connected to the world around you.

The trick to fighting this mental cycle is to convert the energy you're currently using to focus on yourself into energy that is focused outward. This allows you to engage freely with the world, learn more about it through observation, and be present when you connect with others.

HOW TO DEVELOP AN OUTWARD FOCUS

The key to an outward focus is curiosity. Just as you might be curious about what other people think of you, be curious about the world around you.

Don't get caught in the trap of seeing the world through your individual experience. When we're always focused on our own needs, experience, and desires, it makes it that much harder to empathize with people and see the world how it really is. Over time, we develop certain filters that skew our vision of the world from tuning out pieces of it for so long.

To avoid this, we focus outward, always being observant and inquisitive about the world around us.

Be curious about other people, other perspectives, and other situations different from your own. When you feel your energy pulling inward, try to ask a question, validate a response, or show appreciation of someone else.

Maintaining this outward focus helps keep your confidence grounded in reality.

OUTWARD-FOCUSED INTERACTIONS

Sometimes our self-consciousness, nervousness, or excitement can present itself as self-centeredness. When your conversations and interactions with others are filled with statements about yourself, are characterized by long-winded answers, or take up a disproportionate amount of the conversation, it can come across as not being interested in others.

Even with the best intentions, our eagerness, excitement, or self-consciousness might cause a one-sided conversation.

To avoid that, or to redeem a moment, try implementing some of these tactics:

- Listen and ask questions.
- Spend most of your time talking about others.

- Use fewer "I" and "me" statements.
- Take time to tell a complimentary story about someone else.
- Talk about others positively.
- Show appreciation and gratitude.
- Wait before jumping into the conversation; don't be too eager to jump in at the risk of cutting someone off.

CHAPTER EXERCISE: THE INWARD-TO-OUTWARD CONVERSION

The next time you're at a social or professional gathering and you feel your thoughts centering around yourself, try this game:

If you're wondering what other people are thinking about your shirt, convert your inward thought into an outward curiosity about the same topic: *Who else is wearing a conference shirt? I wonder if they've been to this conference before. Maybe I'll strike up a conversation and ask them.*

If you're thinking about sharing a story that you know many people in your group have heard before, try turning the topic outward and sharing the spotlight: *I heard _____ had a great story the other day. Do you mind sharing it with everyone? I really thought that was an awesome thing you did.*

_____

_____

_____

_____

_____

_____

_____

_____

_____

_____

_____

_____

Chapter

15

Invest in Yourself

With only 24 hours in a day, long to-do lists, and an abundance of responsibilities calling out for our time and energy, it can feel like just another chore to add ourselves to the list. But investing in yourself and your abilities is a key component in maintaining and continuing to build your confidence and the skills required for your success.

The time that you set aside for your own growth and development is a true *investment*. How? Well, an investment is not a single transaction. When you invest in yourself, you're not giving your time to an empty void or trading it for a temporary commodity. Instead, you're investing your time to collect a *return* eventually.

Secondly, the value of your investments compounds and grows over time. The more you invest, the more value you can draw from. In this case, your skills and education continue to grow and expand. As a result, they can directly impact the opportunities available to you, the speed at which you accomplish your goals, and the arsenal of skills you can use for various projects.

Rather than feeling guilty for "spending" your time, invest it into a safe bet with a guaranteed return: *you*.

COMMIT TO CONTINUOUS IMPROVEMENT

The growth, development, and maintenance of your skills is best accomplished with continuous practice. To sustain this effort, you need to commit to your own improvement.

With the current pace of technology and the ever-shifting marketplaces, your skills need to be expertly maintained and updated frequently. Don't let your skills get outdated by falling behind in your practice. Instead, make a commitment to yourself to continually improve and practice your skills for the longevity of your career and the achievement of your goals.

DEDICATE TIME TO YOURSELF EACH DAY

Having a dedicated time every day that's just for you can keep your energy and inspiration tanks full. I suggest picking the same time each day to continue the improvement and development of your skills and to stay informed on any news and trends in your industry.

For me, this time is in the morning. I love having quiet alone time first thing to start my day learning about my field. I read books and articles or watch videos to learn something new each day. The magic of this strategy lies in the brevity and consistency of making it a practice to invest in yourself.

KNOW YOU'RE WORTH IT

I know it can be hard to carve out just a few moments of your day for yourself. Some of us might even feel guilty for setting aside time to focus on ourselves *every day*. But remember, this is an investment with a return that can benefit every other aspect of your life. Believe in yourself and make the investment. You are absolutely worth it.

CHAPTER EXERCISE: INVESTMENT TIME

Look at your schedule and pick a window of at least ten minutes that you can dedicate solely to yourself each day. Make a commitment to show up, and reward yourself for doing so.

This time is yours to invest into the skills that can propel you forward. It can include a practice of meditation to refuel your energy and keep you focused or reading one chapter each day so you make consistent and steady progress on your reading list.

Over time, this investment will produce a profitable return that will keep your skills and knowledge relevant to enable you to reach new levels of success.

_____

_____

_____

_____

_____

_____

_____

_____

_____

_____

_____

_____

_____

_____

Chapter

16

Find Mentors

Even the most confident people don't achieve their goals on their own. Behind the most successful people is a team of family, friends, colleagues, and mentors who helped get them there. Setting yourself up for success includes leveraging your internal and external networks to find a mentor who can help guide you on your journey.

WHAT DOES A MENTOR DO?

A mentor is someone in your corner who has walked a similar path before you. They serve as a role model and a safe place for you to talk about your goals and dreams. Their guidance and one-on-one professional development based on their own experience can make this one of the most valuable relationships in your personal network.

There are two main types of mentorships to explore: skill-based mentorships and career mentorships. You should always be looking for mentors to fill each of these roles, even though you might need one more than the other at different points in your career.

SKILL-BASED MENTORS

Skill-based mentors are the resource you go to when you're looking to build your skills or get them to the next level. Books, courses, and coaches can only do so much in skill-based learning, but leadership from a mentor who is an expert in a specific skill you're trying to develop can give you the context, insight, and experience to gain the deeper understanding you need.

One beneficial way to learn from a skill-based mentor is to shadow them. This allows you to see their skills in action and have the opportunity to ask questions that provide insight into how they choose to use that skill.

This type of knowledge can't be transferred from a book, classroom, or online course. With skill-based mentoring, you can see the real-world application of the skill at hand.

CAREER MENTORS

While a skill-based mentor can range from brief to seasonal, you should be looking to nurture a long-term relationship with a career mentor. Find someone who's been where you want to go and has had a similar path to get there. Choose someone who understands your individual situation and the challenges that lie ahead of you.

A great career mentor can confidently help you navigate the twists and turns of your career with valuable insight and wisdom.

HOW TO FIND A MENTOR

The first place to look for a mentor is in your network. Strategically comb through your current network for someone you think can help you level up in your career.

Be as clear and specific as possible about what you want to learn before you search for a mentor. Be sure to discuss your expectations ahead of time, and be clear on the goals of the mentorship to maximize its success.

CHAPTER EXERCISE: FINDING A MENTOR

Referring to the weaknesses previously listed (in the chapter 5 exercise) that you'd like to grow and develop, choose a skill on which you'd like to improve. Write down specific things you'd like to learn within that skill, then list different places you might find a skill-based mentor to help you.

Look at your vision statement and your career objectives. Think of the areas in which you might need help from a mentor along your journey. Then, brainstorm places you might find a career mentor—including in your network and organization. Be selective and choose someone with whom you can envision a long-term mentorship.

_____

_____

_____

_____

_____

_____

_____

_____

_____

_____

_____

_____

_____

_____

_____

_____

Chapter

17

Establish a Daily Practice

In all things—and especially in confidence—establishing a daily practice ensures that core concepts and fundamental principles are applied to the activities of your day-to-day life. This is how we create positive habits and form a life that supports the vision for our future and our journey through confidence.

One area that often disrupts this path is stress. Whether it's a demanding work environment, a full plate of household chores and responsibilities, or the list of expectations we've placed on ourselves, we can feel stressed and overwhelmed when we fail to complete our to-do list or fall behind.

To prevent stress from derailing our confident progress, we can incorporate a daily practice into our lives that instills a healthy work-life balance.

THE ELUSIVE WORK-LIFE BALANCE

There are some people who seem to keep it all together at work, handle stressful tasks with a smile, and have a fulfilling life outside of work. How do they do it?

The key to a balanced life lies in prioritization and intention. It's not that these individuals have more hours in a day than the rest of us, but they typically have firm boundaries around how they spend their time so they can be fully present in whatever they're doing.

When you work with intention and presence, you eliminate distractions and multitasking and work more efficiently. When it's time to be at home, you're completely present and intentional in your leisure so you can refuel and recharge with activities that bring you joy. Rather than incorporating your work life into your home responsibilities or worrying about chores in the back of your mind while you're working, you remain focused on the task in front of you and trust that you will complete the rest when it's time to focus on them.

The key to balance is having clear boundaries around what is most important to you and protecting them in your daily practice.

LIFE HAPPENS FOR YOU, NOT TO YOU

In all aspects of your life, *you* are in the driver's seat. Every person on the planet gets the same 24 hours in a day, and you *decide* what you do with yours.

Sometimes we want to blame circumstances for interfering with our lives and blame our stress on outside factors. While obstacles and situational circumstances can indeed be stressful, we ultimately decide what we do with that stress. We can either channel it into complaining, procrastinating, and dreading the task at hand, or we can welcome the challenge, find an opportunity within it, and tackle it with intention and enthusiasm. When you relinquish power over your own life, a powerless view of the world swiftly follows. It's as if life happens *to* you, rather than *for* you.

Be intentional in your decisions and sacrifices. Own your choices, and be confident in the power you have over your life.

CHAPTER EXERCISE: WHAT REALLY MATTERS AT THE END OF THE DAY

The legacy we leave is not about what we do but who we are. At the end of each day, only three things matter:

1. Was I true to myself?

2. Did I invest in myself?

3 Did I move myself forward?

Instead of thinking about the tasks in the day ahead or the things you didn't finish today, reflect on the things you accomplished. Think of the problems you tackled and the choices you made to stick to your core values. Allow yourself to feel proud for being true to yourself, investing in yourself, and moving yourself forward each day.

_____

_____

_____

_____

_____

_____

_____

_____

_____

_____

_____

_____

_____

_____

Chapter

18

You Are the Average of the Five People with Whom You Spend the Most Time

There's a lot of truth to Jim Rohn's famous quote: "You are the average of the five people you spend the most time with." Numerous studies have shown the impact and influence that your relationships have on your self-esteem, outlook on life, and decision-making.

The belief systems we hold about ourselves and the world around us are shaped by those closest to us. So it's important to be intentional about the people you choose to include in your life: Do they encourage you to move forward, or are they holding you back?

AVOID NEGATIVE PEOPLE

We don't always realize the effect of negative messages on our thoughts and actions. But when the people around you are constantly complaining about their lives, or the messages from television and the media are judgmental and negative, you'll start to notice the same negative language appearing in your own words and inner thoughts.

Be conscious of the energy and focus people are bringing into your life and compare it with your core values. Do you feel inspired to move ahead and tackle problems after spending time with certain friends? Avoid spending time with those who are negative and don't take control over their own lives. This is a contagious mentality that can derail you from your path of success.

SPEND YOUR TIME
WITH POSITIVE PEOPLE

In contrast, if you want a positive attitude and outlook, surround yourself with positive people. Find the people in your life and network who are upbeat and enthusiastic—even when less than ideal circumstances or obstacles appear.

When the people around you are constantly celebrating the actions and achievements of those around them with a fun and positive attitude, you can't help but do the same!

SURROUND YOURSELF
WITH SUCCESSFUL PEOPLE

By now, you probably know where this point is heading: if you want to be successful in your life, spend your time with those who are successful.

Successful individuals stand out from the crowd. In addition to typically having a more positive and can-do attitude, they also have proven their ability to overcome obstacles and push through for their own success.

Spend your time with people you can learn from and who inspire you to be successful.

BE ONE OF THE FIVE FOR SOMEONE ELSE

One of the best ways to practice and learn something is to teach it. Aim to be one of the five positive and successful people in someone else's life. Help others in their own journey and share any helpful insights or wisdom you've gained so far.

With each of us on our own individual path, helping others to be successful doesn't take any space away from your own journey. Choose to be a positive and inspirational force in the world around you.

CHAPTER EXERCISE: KNOW YOUR FIVE

Take the next few weeks to objectively observe the people you spend your time with. Are there individuals who leave you drained and exhausted? Are there people who inspire and encourage you or make you want to lunge forward in confidence? Are the majority of a person's comments optimistic and uplifting or negative and discouraging?

Take mental notes of your interactions with these individuals and the way you feel after spending time with them, and compare how their values align with the traits you want to cultivate within yourself. Use that information to make conscious decisions about the people you spend your time with.

Chapter

Find Your Voice

Having the loudest voice has nothing to do with volume and *everything* to do with conviction. Your voice is a critical tool that shapes others' perception of you, drives your communication, and determines the level of respect others hold for you.

The strength of your voice comes from its authenticity. A voice powered by confidence and authenticity can be a catalyst for change. A voice rooted in self-consciousness or shallowness—no matter how loud—is easy to ignore.

FINDING YOUR AUTHENTIC VOICE

The authority of your voice lies in your connection to yourself. There is no one else like you, and no one else can speak for the thoughts, ideas, or convictions you hold in your mind except for you. The closer your voice is in alignment with your core values, the stronger it will be.

ASK FOR WHAT YOU WANT

No matter how well you think someone knows you or sees your efforts, you can't expect anyone to know what goes on inside your mind—including the things you want. Communicating and asking for what you want is the only way to make your requests known. When you make a request rooted in authenticity that aligns with your core values, it is more likely to be seriously considered.

Remember, being confident and asking for what you want is a lot different than barging in and demanding what you think you deserve. The latter is a result of giving your power to outside influences and handing the keys to another driver. Contrastingly, asking for what you want with full confidence relieves you from the belief that anyone owes you anything. You must take ownership of your requests and communicate them with full responsibility and control.

PRACTICE USING YOUR VOICE

The way we learn to use our voice is greatly influenced by our early environments and experiences. For some, speaking up for oneself is foreign and uncomfortable. For others, they might think that they need to be the loudest voice in the room to be heard.

Wherever you might lie on the spectrum, your voice is a skill that can be trained and developed. Like all skills, it must be practiced.

To practice using your voice in new ways, start with small steps. Practice in a safe and controlled environment around people who care about you. Be vulnerable and let them know what you're working on so they can join you in celebrating your progress. Have patience and compassion for yourself and know that you can develop and fine-tune this skill throughout your entire life. Over time, you'll be able to communicate effectively with palpable authenticity and make a positive impact with your unique voice.

SPEAK WITH CONFIDENCE

Equally important to finding your authentic voice is knowing when and how to act on it. Just remember that whenever your voice is aligned with your core values, it is valuable. Learn to use it confidently to advocate for yourself and your beliefs. It doesn't require a perfect performance or bravado to be taken seriously. Your voice is uniquely yours, and that makes it worth being heard.

CHAPTER EXERCISE: PREPARE YOUR VOICE

Think of a recent situation where you wish you had communicated or used your voice differently. From this observation, pick one skill that would have improved that interaction.

Maybe it's asking for what you want without apologizing or slowing down your communication to avoid interrupting. Whatever aspect of your voice you'd like to improve, make a conscious effort to further develop it, and practice using your voice in confidence.

_____

_____

_____

_____

_____

_____

_____

_____

_____

_____

_____

_____

_____

_____

_____

_____

Chapter

Focus on the Future and Forgive the Past

Focus is a quiet and magical tool that has the ability to propel us forward if it is pointed at our future or keep us in place when it is centered on the past. Whichever we choose to focus on expands and consumes our view, eventually pushing out everything else. That's why it's so important that we use this technique to keep our sights on the positive future ahead.

FORGIVING THE PAST

The past has been lived through and is finished and complete. There is nothing in the past for you except for the lessons you take from it.

Forgiving your mistakes and letting go of the past will relieve you from feeling compelled to look over your shoulder while on your journey toward your future. Do your part by tying off any open threads that no longer serve you and finding closure for any issues in your past. This can take some work, but it's worth it.

If we let our focus slip to the past, it can trap us and keep us there for an indefinite amount of time. Whatever is in your past, choose to forgive and let it go.

LOOKING THROUGH THE OBSTACLES

The most successful people are continuously focused on the reasons why they will succeed. There's no time to focus on the past when you're moving ahead so purposefully.

Part of this focus is developing the ability to look through obstacles when they appear. You want to train your vision to be so strong that it's like an X-ray. No obstacle can stand in your way when you can walk right through it.

This kind of mentality doesn't allow any obstacle to stop you or slow you down.

FOCUS IS A PRACTICE

It's a simple concept, but implementing a sharp laser focus is harder than it looks. To keep your focus centered, you need a clear vision of where you want to be and what you hope to achieve. Without this, the rest of the picture is blurry. It's hard to move swiftly when you can't see very far ahead.

The practice of focus requires persistence. There are plenty of things in the periphery just waiting to grab your attention and steal your focus. Know that they exist, and if you veer off course, recover quickly and regain focus on your vision. Your diligence and perseverance will pay off.

KEEP THE FOCUS BRIGHT

In addition to keeping your focus on the future, you also want to stay focused on the positives. Even if your sights are set on the future but you focus on the potential negative outcomes or the mistakes you might make, you'll end up moving at a crawling speed in the dark toward your goal.

Be confident in your vision. Focus on the upside, the silver linings, and the positive and bright future ahead of you. Whatever you choose to focus on will determine where you end up being.

CHAPTER EXERCISE: RELENTLESS VISION

Review the vision statement you wrote for yourself. Close your eyes and create a clear, detailed scene of what that looks like.

Now pick a short-term goal that moves you forward toward this vision.

In your daily life, make it a practice to envision your future and the immediate objective ahead of you. Try this exercise when you need a little extra motivation to push through an obstacle or when you're in the middle of a long set of mundane tasks. Pull up this vision and remind yourself why you're doing this and where you're going to be.

_____

_____

_____

_____

_____

_____

_____

_____

_____

_____

_____

_____

_____

_____

_____

Chapter

21

Commit to Becoming an Expert in Your Chosen Field

The next step to leveling up in your confidence journey and accelerating your path to success is to become an expert in your chosen field. Not only does this help you cultivate and specialize your skills, but it also creates opportunities that lead to success.

HOW TO BECOME AN EXPERT

Being an expert means that you know more about your industry, market, and unique offering than anyone else. It also means that your performance in the field of your expertise is superior and you have the numbers to back it up.

As you can imagine, this isn't an overnight process. Becoming an expert takes time and diligence, but the time and energy that you put into this process has a multitude of benefits.

While you're on your path to becoming an expert, you'll soak in new information and further develop your skills. These will create opportunities even before you're a qualified expert and will support your attainment of the vision for your life. These efforts are propelling you forward in the same direction but with the added benefit of becoming a trusted expert—which will bring even more opportunity.

KNOW YOUR EXPERTISE

You should be able to sum up your expertise, your profession, and the value you bring to your field in just one line. Some people call it an elevator pitch, but I like to call it a communication line because it better describes what you're doing: you're communicating what you do.

Your chosen expertise should align with your vision for your life. Putting those two concepts together in a concise and memorable way creates a communication line that's easy to repeat and share with others.

Consider this: you're at an event and someone asks what you do. If you share a couple paragraphs' worth of information about what you do, why you do it, how it started, and what you're planning to do in the future, that person might be really excited and interested in the moment. But when they walk away and someone else asks who you are, it's a lot of work to recall which pieces of information sum up who you are.

Instead, have a brief and memorable line that sums it all up and can be repeated easily. Just having this one line can lead to more opportunities to share your expertise.

WHY BECOME AN EXPERT?

The path to becoming an expert requires an abundance of skills and dedication that ultimately will help you on your path to success.

Whether you choose to become a widely known expert and speaker in your craft or you're just known in your field and community as an expert, it doesn't matter. Once you are an expert in your chosen field, you've equipped yourself with the skills to excel and placed yourself ahead of the competition with your superior performance.

From this alone, you will have more opportunities and enjoy more success.

CHAPTER EXERCISE: YOUR COMMUNICATION LINE

Answer the following questions to create your unique communication line:

- What is your name and profession?

  _____

  _____

- What value do you add to your field? (What makes you unique?)

  _____

  _____

- What problem can you solve?

  _____

  _____

- What benefit do you provide?

  _____

  _____

From these answers, create a concise version that can be remembered easily by the people you meet.

_____

_____

_____

_____

_____

_____

_____

Chapter

22

Energy In Produces Energy Out

Taking care of yourself physically, mentally, spiritually, and emotionally will help you build and maintain your energy to be used in your work, passions, or life's mission. The better you are at managing your energy, the more energy you'll have to put toward your work and passions.

MAINTAIN A HEALTHY LIFESTYLE

Eating well, exercising, and getting an adequate amount of sleep are absolutely vital to your success. Some people think this is optional—that they can operate without as much sleep as everyone else or get by on a minimally nutritious diet. The truth is, while the body might be able to function temporarily on an unhealthy lifestyle, it's not sustainable. When you are consistently withdrawing from your body's energy, eventually it's going to ask for a deposit.

If you're not adequately maintaining your health, you leave yourself susceptible to illness, burnout, exhaustion, and a myriad of other problems. This is not an item that you can afford to put off. Establish a healthy lifestyle now and make your wellness a priority.

DO WHAT YOU LOVE

If you're doing what you love, it really doesn't feel like work. Pursuing our passions refuels our energy stores, and when that's aligned with the work we do, we get to live in an invigorating and inspiring cycle.

Spend time doing the things that bring you joy and fill up your emotional tank. Make time to pursue a hobby, appreciate and see art, or connect with nature. Wherever you find your source of inspirational energy, make it a practice to be there. When we're connected to our passions, we feel a greater sense of purpose that allows us to confidently pursue the vision for our life.

MANAGE YOUR ENERGY, NOT YOUR TIME

Time is finite, meaning there are only so many hours in the day and there is nothing you can do to change that.

However, you *do* have control over your energy. You can refuel your energy tank, deplete it, and manage its stores based on the things you do, the people you're with, and the avenues you pursue.

Don't rely on others to refuel you. Find a practice, a passion, or something you can connect with that you can pursue when your energy stores are low. This allows you to continue to move forward in confidence and not feel trapped or stuck by needing to find a fuel source.

Know that you are your own fuel source and you already have everything you need within you.

When you're an expert at managing your energy, you learn how to "do more with less." You can accomplish more and have greater stamina to continue on your path forward when your energy stores are maintained and controlled by you.

CHAPTER EXERCISE: FIND YOUR FUEL STATIONS

Make a list of things that give you energy. Consider activities—like going for a hike, taking a bath, listening to music, or working out—and places that fill up your tank when you're feeling low.

List all the things you can think of that you can do when your energy starts to feel low. Keep this list handy when you need a little extra inspiration to refuel your tank and get back on your path to greatness.

_____

_____

_____

_____

_____

_____

_____

_____

_____

_____

_____

_____

_____

_____

_____

_____

_____

_____

_____

Chapter

Look the Part

If you want others to believe in what you do, you need to look and feel the part. Our posture, clothing, body language, and facial expressions all play a role in how others perceive us. In fact, 55 percent of a person's first impression of us is based solely on our appearance. That means that before we even get to meet and talk with someone, they've already created a majority of their opinion about us.

This is why looking the part is important. It opens up more opportunities for you, whether in your career, your network, or your personal life.

FIRST IMPRESSIONS

Within the first 30 seconds of meeting someone, they've already made their mind up about you. They've likely decided if they want to get to know you better, collaborate, or make an effort to start a friendship. They deduce all of this information based on very little information about you. So how do you make a good first impression?

1. **Be positive:** People enjoy spending their time with positive people.

2. **Be inviting and approachable:** Be warm and inviting in your interactions and attentive to what others are sharing.

3. **Keep an outward focus:** Talk less about yourself, and ask more questions about others.

STAY ON BRAND

Your personal brand helps people recognize you, remember you, and easily recall what you stand for. To stay on brand, the most important component is to be consistent. When you're driven by your core values, this shouldn't be a problem. Be mindful to consistently align all the outlets of your personal brand. These include your personal interactions, work interactions, social media, interviews, speaking engagements, social engagements, and so on. The things you do and say should remain consistent regardless of where you are or whom you're with.

Secondly, make sure your physical appearance supports your brand. If you are working to establish yourself as a professional expert and business consultant for companies, it's important that you look like a professional expert in appropriate business attire. The same principle is true for any career.

CHAPTER EXERCISE: BUILD YOUR PERSONAL BRAND

You've aligned your core values, defined the vision for your life, and outlined your strengths and weaknesses. Building your personal brand puts these items together to create a cohesive and consistent experience of who you are whenever you interact with people.

1. **Be clear about your passions:** Use them to circle back and share your life's journey and mission with others.

2. **Tell a story:** In addition to having a concise communication line, have a brand story with 2–3 sentences that cover the events and circumstances that made you who you are and put you on this journey.

3. **Update your online brand:** Find a way to present yourself as a well-rounded individual. This might mean adding more of your personal life and passions into your business interactions or updating your personal profile to be more professional.

As with all things, root your personal brand in your authenticity and watch it grow.

Chapter

A Habit of Gratitude

It's important to make a habit out of practicing gratitude (even on days that *aren't* Thanksgiving). Gratitude is a powerful mental tool that causes us to see more positive things in our lives.

Studies have shown that a practice of gratitude leads to being happier and more fulfilled. It's also been proven to help with trauma, stress, and anxiety. And if *that* wasn't enough, gratitude can be a catalyst for rewarding and fulfilling relationships.

Here's how to shift your mental energy and train your mind to practice a habit of gratitude.

SHIFT YOUR THINKING TO THE PRESENT

When we get too far ahead in our thoughts worrying about the things we need to do or get stuck in the past thinking about the things we didn't get done, we lose sight of the present—and that's where gratitude lives.

Having a habit of gratitude is about focusing on the present and pointing out the good things in our lives right now. When we focus on the present, we can be more intentional with our actions and keep our thoughts centered.

THINK POSITIVE

Thinking positively is easier for some than others, but everyone is able to "catch" negative thoughts and turn them into positive ones—it's all a matter of practice.

Research by the psychologist Barbara Fredrickson has shown that gratitude broadens and builds the brain's capacity to overcome negative emotional states. This goes beyond thinking about positive things over negative things. For those who regularly practice gratitude and seek out positivity, they also have more ideas in creative brainstorming than their counterparts.

Commit to a daily practice of gratitude to train your mind to see things more positively. When you find yourself repeating negative thoughts, kindly correct them and find something good in your present situation.

TRAIN YOUR FOCUS

Remember how easy it is to create a biased view when our minds have been primed with an idea? In the habit of gratitude, we can use this quirk of our minds to actually train the brain to be more positive.

By priming our mind with regular thoughts of gratefulness, it slowly changes our focus over time. Eventually, it's less work to instill a habit of gratitude, and you'll start to see more and more opportunities to be grateful in the present moment.

CHAPTER EXERCISE: YOUR DAILY PRACTICE OF GRATITUDE

Before you fall asleep each night, take a gratitude break and think of three things that you are grateful for in your life at that moment. It can be something small, like "I was so grateful for those extra ten minutes I got to read today." Or larger things, like "I'm grateful for my job and the security it brings me."

Making gratitude a daily habit will gradually influence your overall outlook on life and make it more positive.

Chapter

Establish Boundaries

The boundaries you set for yourself are closely related to your confidence and self-esteem. When your confidence and self-esteem are high, your boundaries tend to be more defined as well.

Establishing healthy boundaries helps us protect the things most precious to us. These should align with your core values and purpose.

BOUNDARIES: THE BLINDERS TO SUCCESS

We're accustomed to thinking of boundaries as barriers that keep people and things out and away from us. Sometimes boundaries are just blinders for our own personal journey to tune out distractions and stay focused on the path ahead. Don't feel guilty for setting clear boundaries for yourself. Boundaries are essential to your confidence journey and to your future success.

Consider these blinders as protection of your path ahead, and don't invite unnecessary distractions or obstacles.

KNOW WHAT'S WORTH PROTECTING

To establish effective boundaries, you need to know what's worth protecting. This is determined by taking inventory of your vision for your life, your core values, and your relationships.

- **Your goals:** Protect your vision for your life and your path to get there.

- **Your values:** Stand for your non-negotiable core values, and don't let anything interfere with them.

- **Your time and energy:** Be intentional with your time, and don't feel obligated to make commitments that don't serve you or your journey.

- **Your relationships:** Don't let toxicity or negative people interfere with your valued relationships.

- **Your physical space:** Know what makes you uncomfortable, and be confident to speak up for the physical space you need when that boundary is crossed.

Fill your life with things that are fulfilling, positive, and focused on encouragement toward your goals. Those are the things and the people who are worth protecting.

BOUNDARIES CAN BE FIRM AND NICE

There are some of us who might feel bad when we need to stand up for ourselves and establish a clear boundary. If we haven't had much practice, it can feel awkward or mean.

Luckily, boundaries can be firm and respectful at the same time. Communicate your boundary requests respectfully while remaining firm on what you need. When your rejections, denials, or refusals are rooted in your core values, it's harder to take them as a personal offense. If it's authentic to you, show them that you care but that you are unable to fulfill that request. Depending on the nature of the request, you might say that you welcome hearing about similar opportunities in the future.

When you can be firm *and* polite, your requests are more likely to be heard and respected.

THE FREEING POWER OF BOUNDARIES

Although it might seem counterintuitive, the absence of boundaries actually creates a more limited existence. That's because without boundaries, our mind, time, and energy stores become vulnerable to distractions, toxic relationships, and unnecessary commitments.

With boundaries set in confidence, you can experience freedom from the things that don't serve you and protect the time, space, and energy to be intentional with the things worth protecting.

CHAPTER EXERCISE: THE THINGS WORTH PROTECTING

List out all the things in your life worth protecting with firm boundaries. Include items from the physical, mental, and emotional realms.

Keep these things in mind when you are presented with a new opportunity, request, or commitment. Does it infringe on any of your boundaries?

Chapter

26

Find Others Who Believe in You

If we surround ourselves with people who don't have our best interests in mind, we risk eventually being led off course from our own life journey. Finding others who believe in you can be hard to do. However, some of these individuals might be closer than you think.

USE THE SELF-CONFIDENCE OF OTHERS UNTIL YOU CAN ESTABLISH YOUR OWN

Until you are walking through this world in complete confidence (and even after that), you can use the self-confidence of others to grow your own.

Sometimes when we're just getting started in our self-confidence journey, it helps to have people in our corner who believe in us when it's hard to believe in ourselves. This requires a great deal of trust and vulnerability to share these moments with others, but with the right people who are invested in what's best for you (including your success), these positive relationships can be life-changing.

WHO ARE THESE PEOPLE?

To find others who believe in you, you need to know the right traits to look for and be able to recognize individuals who possess them within your circle.

These individuals are **people who are already confident in who they are.** They exude healthy and consistent confidence despite varying circumstances, and their confidence doesn't seem to be influenced by others. Confident people can help you grow without feeling threatened by your success because they know we're all on our own unique journey.

Another place to look is in the **leaders of your organization**. Make a list of people who have advocated for you before you ever felt comfortable advocating for yourself. Who are they? It's likely that they are leaders and superiors at your organization who recognize your hard work and believe in your success. Some of these leaders might be willing to take on a more involved role in your network and be a positive force in your journey toward confidence.

If you already have a mentor, lean into that relationship and receive valuable feedback, insight, and pep talks when you need an extra push from someone who believes in you.

WHY DOES IT MATTER?

So much of confidence is tied to belief. When that belief in ourselves is new and unfamiliar, it seems unnatural to tell ourselves some of the mantras and phrases we say to ourselves in confidence.

For the time being, having an influential circle of people who believe in you can help solidify your mind's reasoning for developing your own confidence. This stage is meant to be temporary until you get your confidence efforts off the ground.

These are valuable relationships. Be sure to express your gratitude and make these connections mutually beneficial in some way if you can.

CHAPTER EXERCISE: FIND YOUR BELIEVERS

Reflect on the connections in your life and the people in your network. Do any individuals stand out to you as confident people who have advocated for you or celebrated your success without any provocation?

Consider making them one of the people in your inner circle. Spend time with them and try to absorb their positive outlook and can-do attitude, which can have a positive and exponential impact on your own outlook.

_____

_____

_____

_____

_____

_____

_____

_____

_____

_____

_____

_____

_____

_____

_____

_____

_____

Chapter

27

Know What You Can and Cannot Control

You have control over two things in your life: your attitude and your actions. Everything else is out of your control.

When you choose to take action on the things within your control, you'll create more opportunities for yourself, work more efficiently, be more successful, and enjoy the life you have. When you let your stress and anxieties consume your mind and your time, you're more likely to experience the negative outcomes you worry about.

INFLUENCE VS. OUTCOME

Your attitude and actions can influence the end result, but they cannot control the outcome. For example, you can control your attitude, how you communicate, and what you put into a relationship, but you can't make a person like you. You can control the effort you put into a competitive project, but you can't control who wins.

You increase your odds of achieving your desired outcome when you use your attitude and actions to influence a situation. You must also release the stress and anxiety of worrying about the outcome, which is out of your control. Be proud of the work you put in and be compassionate to yourself when you experience disappointing outcomes. Regardless of the outcome, always celebrate your actions and effort.

TURN WORRIES INTO CHOICES

Take control over your own stress with your attitude. Turning your worry into a choice is one way to adjust your attitude so that you are motivated to take action. When you have a problem you are worried about, create a list of the possible options, make a choice that aligns with your values, and put your effort into executing the plan.

For example, if you're worried about not having enough time to complete all the things on your to-do list, switch your perspective to see your options for taking control: "We all get 24 hours in a day; I'm choosing what to do with mine."

- "I choose to wake up earlier so that I can get everything done."
- "I choose to be vulnerable and ask for help so that everything gets done."
- "I choose to do whatever I can do to the best of my ability and let go of what can't get done."

By turning your actions into choices, you can enjoy the work you're doing and let go of unnecessary stress. The work gets done either way, but one approach is much more enjoyable than the other.

THE THINGS YOU CAN'T CONTROL

Some of our most common sources of stress are out of our control—things like time, other people, and the environment (the economy, the market, the government, etc.). Accept that you don't have control, and instead focus on how you can influence positive change in your life through your attitude and actions.

CHAPTER EXERCISE: FIND YOUR CONTROL

Think of an area or subject in your life that brings you uncertainty. Make a list of the things you can do to influence the outcome of the situation.

Maybe you're worried about finding a new job. Your list might include applying to one new job every day or spending X minutes/hours each day looking for opportunities, growing your network and connections, learning new skills to bolster your resume, and so on.

Whenever you start to worry about all the possible negative outcomes, put your energy into this actionable list to influence a positive outcome.

_____

_____

_____

_____

_____

_____

_____

_____

_____

_____

_____

_____

_____

_____

_____

_____

_____

_____

_____

_____

_____

_____

_____

_____

_____

_____

_____

_____

_____

_____

_____

_____

_____

_____

_____

_____

_____

_____

_____

_____

_____

_____

_____

Chapter

Take a Risk

You've mapped out your vision, aligned yourself with your core values, and equipped yourself with the tools and strategies you need to succeed in your confidence journey. Now it's time to take the leap. Learn to assess actual risk and imagined risk. You have the power to take action against both.

SUCCESS DOESN'T COME TO YOU

Wouldn't it be nice if you received a gift-wrapped box at your door one day with a note that read, "I've seen your hard work and talent. Here's an opportunity that will bring you guaranteed success"? Unfortunately, that's not how opportunities typically come into our lives.

Opportunities usually present themselves in gritty, less-than-ideal circumstances. They come from sweat and relentless drive, navigating through an unknown place, or discovering something beautiful after cleaning up a mess and getting your hands dirty. Even when the chance at success presents itself in a gift-wrapped box labeled "Opportunity," we tend to point out that the gift wrap is in our least favorite color.

Adopt the perspective that everything is an opportunity and you'll be successful. Success comes from trusting your abilities and taking more opportunities than the average person. That doesn't mean you'll have a 100 percent success rate, but you *will* have a winning record.

OUR BIGGEST FEARS

Our strongest responses of fear are often tied to our deepest desires.

When a scary opportunity arises and you don't feel ready for it, take time to identify where your fear is coming from. What are you scared might happen? What would that mean? What would that threaten? Be connected to your desires so that you can spot these fear responses quickly.

When we get to the root of our fear, we often find our desires. This becomes very true when we're assessing risks. Sometimes the risk that is most intimidating and scary is the one that will fulfill our deepest desires. Know yourself, your fears, and your desires, and take action in confidence.

TAKE THE RISK

When an opportunity arises, trust yourself. Our minds are quick to analyze the potential positive and negative outcomes. You can use these thoughts to *inform* your decision, but assume the responsibility for taking the risk and acting when the time is right.

Have confidence in yourself and your abilities. When you're aligned with your core values, you have every reason to trust yourself, your instincts, and your intuition. Look back at your positive track record and seek to replicate these results.

In all things, keep your focus on the positive and take the leap forward.

CHAPTER EXERCISE: REFLECT ON SUCCESS

Think of a time you took a risk and it paid off. Do you remember how it felt before you took the risk and the worries or concerns you had? Do you remember how those concerns were addressed and resolved in the end?

Reflecting on experiences of success, especially when it comes to taking risks, can help ground us in reality when we're worried about the risks of a new opportunity.

Celebrate your successes and appreciate your own accomplishments, then trust yourself to do the same when the next opportunity comes.

Chapter

Rinse and Repeat

Y ou've made it to the final chapter. I hope this book has empowered you to feel and act more confident in your relationships, career, and ambitions. I have just a few more thoughts to share with you before we close this chapter… and this book.

CONFIDENCE IS FLUID

Just like the changes and adaptations you experience in your life, your confidence and the strategies laid out in this book are fluid and flexible.

Don't expect your current level of confidence always to remain the same. Don't expect it to continue on its steep upward trajectory or be disappointed if it doesn't. Your confidence is fluid: it ebbs and flows; there are high tides and low tides, and sometimes it can feel like you're not moving at all. That's okay. Accept this, be compassionate with yourself always, and get back on the "boat" to continue your journey.

RINSE AND REPEAT

While the core concepts of this book remain consistent, the strategies shared with you are also fluid. We can be leveling up in our confidence journey for our entire lives by working and reworking our values, reassessing our strengths and weaknesses, investing in ourselves, and so on.

The exercises in this book are designed to be revisited and practiced as you navigate change, encounter new opportunities, or face what feels like a plateau. Wherever you are in your journey, these strategies will be here for you.

CHAPTER EXERCISE: CONTINUE YOUR JOURNEY

The book is complete, but the handbook is still available to you on www.ValueSpeaker.com! Refer back to this book as you need. Return to specific exercises or subjects, or revisit your answers within the chapter exercises, to see how much you've grown.

Wishing you all the best on your confidence journey.

About the Author

Meridith Elliott Powell is a business strategist, keynote speaker, and award-winning author with expertise in business growth, sales, and leadership strategies. She was named **One of the Top 15 Business Growth Experts to Watch** by *Currency Fair* and **One of the Top 20 Sales Experts To Follow** by LinkedIn.

A former C-suite executive, Meridith has extensive experience in the banking, health care, and finance industries. She has earned a number of prestigious accreditations, including Master Certified Strategist, Executive Coach and Certified Speaking Professional (a designation held by less than 12% of professional speakers), and Master Certified DISC Trainer and Coach (facilitating and coaching thousands in that program).

Meridith shares her business expertise with organizations through cutting-edge messages rooted in real-life examples and real-world knowledge. She is the author of several books, including *30 Days to Sales Success, Thrive: Strategies to Turn Uncertainty to Competitive Advantage, Winning in the Trust & Value Economy* (USA Best Book Awards finalist), *Own It: Redefining Responsibility—Stories of Power, Freedom & Purpose, The Best Sales Book Ever!* (Nonfiction Authors Association Gold Award recipient), and co-author of *Who Comes Next?: Leadership Succession Planning Made Easy* (Nonfiction Authors Association Gold Award recipient).

www.ValueSpeaker.com

CONTACT

Meridith Elliott Powell

www.ValueSpeaker.com

mere@valuespeaker.com

Office: (828) 243-3510

Toll-Free: (888) 526-9998

Follow Meridith:

MORE BOOKS BY
MERIDITH ELLIOTT POWELL

30 DAYS TO SALES SUCCESS

BUILD MORE PROFITABLE RELATIONSHIPS,
CLOSE MORE SALES, DRIVE MORE BUSINESS

MERIDITH ELLIOTT POWELL, MBA, CSP

WHO COMES NEXT? Leadership Succession Planning Made Easy

"Being able to move seamlessly from one leader to the next is vital for an organization's success. This book is a goldmine of wisdom about succession planning, laid out in a simple-to-apply process."
—Bob Burg | International Best-Selling Coauthor of The Go-Giver Book Series

MARY C. KELLY, PHD | MERIDITH E. POWELL, MBA

THRIVE

"Thrive is a must-read for all who strive to grow intellectually, and to succeed through the opportunities an uncertain world offers."
KEN LANGONE, AMERICAN BILLIONAIRE, PHILANTHROPIST & FOUNDER OF HOME DEPOT

Strategies to Turn Uncertainty to
COMPETITIVE ADVANTAGE

MERIDITH ELLIOTT POWELL
FOREWORD BY TOM FAZIO

AVAILABLE ON AMAZON